A Yummy "Yes" to Life

Delicious Keys to Showing Up For Yourself

by Jessina DeMarco

Foreword by Ruben Mata
International Speaker, Trainer, Author

i

WHAT PEOPLE ARE SAYING ABOUT *A Yummy "Yes" to Life*:

"If you are ready to be inspired and achieve a higher degree of results in your personal or business life, incorporate these weekly affirmations by my friend, Jessina DeMarco. They are very effective."
– K. Lam, Entrepreneur, Tai Chi Master/Instructor

"I have experienced much more happiness, self-confidence and a more complete relationship with myself, with my spouse and children after reading a copy of this incredible Success Guide. It has taught me a lot about myself and helped me get through lots of challenges. Thank You!"
– M. Hernandez, Registered Nurse

"I've had the opportunity to see Jessina grow in leaps and bounds on her life journey and her career launch in the Health and Wellness profession. This publication is a true testament of her personal overcoming and her sharing it with the world to benefit from."
– D. Villalobos, Chiropractor, Wellness Professional

"This book has given me a lot more clarity and self-accountability after reading. By applying these principles, I have had more success in all aspects of my health and family relationships. Thanks Jessina!"
– Pam Andrews, Wife, Stay-At-Home Mom

Editing & Formatting: Dr. Cesar Vargas

Cover Design: Cesar Vargas, Ph.D.

VIP – Veritas Invictus Publishing

8502 East Chapman Avenue | # 302
Orange, California 92869

ISBN 978-1-939180-03-2

jessina@jessinademarco.com

DEDICATION

This book is dedicated to honorable friends who have supported me on my journey of challenge to victorious triumph!

To Marisa Nakhi, my amazing Financial Success Coach. You have facilitated me on my journey of self-discovery from the inside out. It was by divine appointment we crossed paths, and I am ever so grateful for you. One of your best saying that enlightened me forever is, "What is possible for anyone, is possible for me!" Thank you so much, dear, for your love, friendship and support!

To Ruben Mata, my inspirational Life-Empowering Mentor. Through your guided support and impactful teachings, you have exemplified that All things are truly possible and I can be the best Me! Adopting your sound, yet profound, life philosophies has literally transformed every aspect of my life. You constantly remind me of the P's, "Patience, Persistence, and remaining Positive!" Thank you so much for setting a higher standard for what I never perceived possible for me!

To Isabel Apodaca, my beautiful Spiritual Mother. I am eternally grateful and appreciative of you, dear. Your taking me under your wings, giving me hope and faith at the lowest season of my life are gestures of love, which I will cherish and keep present with me for all of my days. Your unconditional dedication to my success in all areas of my life has been instrumental in molding me into who I AM today.

I am extremely blessed and filled with overflowing gratitude for my wonderful Inspirers and Leaders who God has placed in my path and given me favor with. I'm in much appreciation for having God in my life, optimum health, blessed friends & family and for the gift of Life itself! I wouldn't trade any of my life experiences for anything. They have designed me into the unique and Beautiful Light I am today!

~ Jessina DeMarco

ACKNOWLEDGEMENTS

There are a great number of people I'd love to thank for being a part of my life, who have offered and have blessed me with tremendous support along my wonderful journey in experiencing challenges to triumph!

My beautiful family: James (Father), Carolyn (Mom), Kimlyn, Veronica and Vicky (Sisters), Jahi (Brother), Paul (Son)

Honorable Role Models: Ruben Mata, Isabel Apodaca, Marisa Nakhi, Thach Nguyen, Adam Alavi, Chris Bolger, David Dang Vu, Jeremy McGilvrey, Kin Lam, and Van Teodosio.

Life Inspirers: Abraham Hicks, Les Brown, John C. Maxwell, Michael Bernard Beckwith, Rhonda Byrne, Jeff Olson, Ruben Mata, Hector LaMarque, Joel Osteen, Joyce Meyer, Ivan Misner, Thach Nguyen.

If I missed anyone of note, please know that you hold a unique place in my heart.

My beautiful English Springer Spaniel doggie, Lexie! I will always love you girl, through eternity!

TABLE OF CONTENTS
&

$\mathcal{F}$OREWORD

BY RUBEN MATA

C8

I FIRST MET JESSINA AT AN EVENT WHERE I WAS SPEAKING. She had reached out and asked if I would be speaking any other time soon, because she was feeling ill. I replied, "No, I will be traveling out of state and overseas." She said, "OK, I will make it."

To my surprise, Jessina showed up even though she wasn't feeling well. I can remember her smile that lit up the room and the positive energy she shared with everyone around her, and many reciprocated.

Then, after speaking with her, I realized her commitment of keeping her word and showing up, even though she wasn't feeling well.

When you get an opportunity to meet Jessina, you will enjoy her caring attitude, her drive for helping people and, yes, her huge heart.

She has overcome her own life struggles, and found the motivation to do so by looking inside for courage, strength and the will to be more, do more, and share more. The book you have in your hands is her amazing result.

You can rest assured knowing that Jessina walks her talk, and you will benefit of her insights, wisdom and inspiration that she has gathered over the years, which she now shares with you in this book.

As you read these pages and Jessina's reflections, you'll feel as she is speaking directly to you. You may wonder, *how does she know what I'm going through?* Now you will gain clarity and have a map to success to the New You.

As I say in my recent book, STAND, do the best in all you do and you're destined to go "All the Way to the Top."

Now you have the tools and format of how to get there with Jessina's amazing wisdom and simple, yet powerful, life-changing system.

Enjoy your Journey to all your new success!

Ruben Mata
International Speaker, World Peace Ambassador, Author
www.StandWithRuben.com

THE FORMAT

♋

The intention of this workbook is for daily use and application. Your daily activity and participation will assist you in obtaining the results that you desire.

Each week you will receive an inspirational quote, along with my reflection of that thought, idea, concept or philosophy. The object in this is for you to apply this quote as to how it resonates in your personal life.

Just like in life, your results will be in direct proportion to the effort you invest in it.

Be sure to make this a fun adventure! It starts right now! The goal is to see how far you've progressed. Starting with today's date, schedule in your planner, calendar, etc., 11 months from now, to order your next book, and excitingly do it all over again!

I'd definitely like to hear from you with any positive reports or shares on your venture. Feel free to email me your comments and a summary of your progress to **jessina@jessinademarco.com**.

ꝹNTRODUCTION

❦

CONGRATULATIONS! You have taken the first step toward your success and achievement journey. One thing that I can highly emphasize is that you keep this very simple.

By applying these powerful principles, literally, I have been able to change my life from tragedies to victorious and triumphant wins!

As you begin your success journey, read the weekly quote and ask yourself these basic questions:

- ✓ Why am I applying this in my life?
- ✓ What are the steps I'm going to take with this quote?
- ✓ How am I going to apply these basic steps in my day?
- ✓ How do I know I have accomplished my goals?

You may be saying to yourself, "This seems like a lot of work." That's OK. Initially, I thought the same thing. This small daily discipline will cause compounding positive shifts that you probably could never imagine.

I activate and implement these quotes daily, and it has given me the confidence, posture and esteem to believe that anything is truly possible!

Yes and Yes! Let's Begin!

WEEK 1

☙

If your intention is to manifest healing in any area of life, focus on what it FEELS like to have great health or optimal sufficiency in that area! Putting thoughts and energy on the condition or situation itself will only attract more of it! ...I see myself as who I was created to be, Whole and Well!!

Jessina DeMarco

Focus this week on what it feels like to have health and happiness in every area of your life.

Monday: _____

_____

_____

_____

_____

Tuesday: _____

_____

_____

_____

Wednesday: _____

_____

_____

_____

Thursday: _____

_____

_____

_____

Friday: _____

_____

_____

_____

Saturday/Week-In-Review: _____

_____

_____

_____

_____

_____

WEEK 2

☙

*Create an abundance of optimism, compassion and kindness
that uplifts and illuminates the world around you! Intently
look for ways to positively contribute to others lives!...
This positive ripple effect of energy has a way of coming back
around!*

Jessina DeMarco

I will, with intention, be positive at all times to myself and others
around me. I will find ways, big or small, to bless people's lives
selflessly, with no agenda.

Monday: _____

_____

_____

_____

Tuesday: _____

_____

_____

_____

Wednesday: _____

_____

_____

_____

Thursday: _____

_____

_____

_____

Friday: _____

_____

_____

_____

Saturday/Week-In-Review: _____

_____

_____

_____

_____

_____

Week 3

CB

In deep appreciation today for the gift of selfless giving! Begin to give to others, with no agenda! Make everything genuinely about them, and not about yourself. Give this gift daily and joy, happiness, peace and prosperity will show up in your life in miraculous ways!

Jessina DeMarco

This week I will find selfless ways to show appreciation toward others. I will keep in mind that all giving and contributing should be done out of a kind heart with no agenda.

Monday: _____

_____

_____

_____

Tuesday: _____

_____

_____

_____

Wednesday: _____

_____

_____

_____

Thursday: _____

_____

_____

_____

Friday: _____

_____

_____

_____

Saturday/Week-In-Review: _____

_____

_____

_____

_____

WEEK 4

☙

Inner Peace is the most sought after human desire, and we already possess it within! It's a beautiful presence that is never an absence!

Jessina DeMarco

I will set my focus on finding peace in every situation or circumstance, knowing that it's already in me.

Monday: _____

_____

_____

_____

_____

Tuesday: _____

_____

_____

_____

_____

Wednesday: _____

_____

_____

_____

Thursday: _____

_____

_____

_____

Friday: _____

_____

_____

_____

Saturday/Week-In-Review: _____

_____

_____

_____

_____

_____

WEEK 5

☙

Always do your best! What you plant now, you will harvest later. Even if you cannot see the fruits of your labor right away, always know that cultivation is always in the works!

Jessina DeMarco

This week I will focus on doing everything to the best of my ability, knowing that I will be rewarded very well.

Monday: _____

_____

_____

_____

_____

Tuesday: _____

_____

_____

_____

_____

Wednesday: _____

_____

_____

_____

Thursday: _____

_____

_____

_____

Friday: _____

_____

_____

_____

Saturday/Week-In-Review: _____

_____

_____

_____

_____

_____

WEEK 6

❧

As we shift into greater degrees of development, we must make space for the new! We must identify with what it is that's holding us hostage. Until we remove unserving things and associations from the cup, we can't fill it with anything else!

Jessina DeMarco

I will focus this week on what it is that is holding me back to achieve my desired wins. I will pay better attention to what I can remove from my life that is no longer serving my highest and best good.

Monday: _____

_____

_____

_____

Tuesday: _____

_____

_____

_____

Wednesday: _____

_____

_____

_____

Thursday: _____

_____

_____

_____

Friday: _____

_____

_____

_____

Saturday/Week-In-Review: _____

_____

_____

_____

_____

_____

WEEK 7

Leaders are made, not born! Harness and develop your passion, the right people will find you!

Jessina DeMarco

I will focus on what I do best and practice on perfecting my skills and gifts in those areas. I have no need to look for the right people to show up; they will.

Monday: _____

_____

_____

_____

_____

Tuesday: _____

_____

_____

_____

Wednesday: _____

_____

_____

_____

Thursday: _____

_____

_____

_____

Friday: _____

_____

_____

_____

Saturday/Week-In-Review: _____

_____

_____

_____

_____

_____

WEEK 8

❧

Knowing who we truly are and coming into awareness of our higher being is such an amazing discovery! Most people equate who they are with what they do. When casually asking an individual who they are, you will typically get a response regarding their profession or what they do for a living. Who we are and what we do are two completely different things. Our contribution to humanity through works, however that may show up or look like, is merely an overflowing byproduct of our bigger self! The question "Who am I?" opens up to a realm of unconstructed possibilities. Know who you are and you will do what you do even better!

Jessina DeMarco

I choose to discover my higher and bigger self. This will allow me to contribute even more to what I do.

Monday: _____

_____

_____

Tuesday: _____

_____

_____

Wednesday: _____

_____

_____

_____

Thursday: _____

_____

_____

_____

Friday: _____

_____

_____

_____

Saturday/Week-In-Review: _____

_____

_____

_____

_____

_____

WEEK 9

❦

Leaders don't create followers, they create more leaders! Be in great gratitude for the people who create the best in you and causes you to be a great example to others!

Jessina DeMarco

I will be my best in all that I do and keep within my sphere people who stretch and expand me.

Monday: _____

_____

_____

_____

_____

Tuesday: _____

_____

_____

_____

_____

Wednesday: _____

_____

_____

_____

Thursday: _____

_____

_____

_____

Friday: _____

_____

_____

_____

Saturday/Week-In-Review: _____

_____

_____

_____

_____

_____

WEEK 10

☙

View completed chapters of your life not as an end, but a graceful shift into a higher state of awareness! From these life lessons, we gain a better degree of clarity and understanding. Bless and thank situations and experiences. They are only present to anchor us into a more solid foundation! Remember that everything happens in God's divine order!

Jessina DeMarco

This week is choose to focus on what's yet to come in my amazing future and use the past a lessons learned to propel me to where I need to be!

Monday: _____

_____

_____

_____

Tuesday: _____

_____

_____

_____

Wednesday: _____

_____

_____

_____

Thursday: _____

_____

_____

_____

Friday: _____

_____

_____

_____

Saturday/Week-In-Review: _____

_____

_____

_____

_____

_____

*W*EEK 11

⚉

I'm worthy of love, success and happiness! It is my God-given gift to enjoy abundant and overflowing love, success and happiness, which brings the highest level of peace into my life!

Jessina DeMarco

I am worthy of all the best God has for me and I will operate in this divine space of living and being.

Monday: _____

_____

_____

_____

_____

Tuesday: _____

_____

_____

_____

_____

Wednesday: _____

_____

_____

_____

Thursday: _____

_____

_____

_____

Friday: _____

_____

_____

_____

Saturday/Week-In-Review: _____

_____

_____

_____

_____

$\mathcal{W}$EEK 12

❧

True happiness starts with love and acceptance of self! I am the most important person to myself. As I take care of me, I am able to be a bigger blessing and light to others.

Jessina DeMarco

I will make a conscious effort to love and care for myself in every way possible. I know that as I love on myself, it will create higher esteem, which will open up expansion into new possibilities.

Monday: _____

_____

_____

_____

Tuesday: _____

_____

_____

_____

Wednesday: _____

_____

_____

_____

Thursday: _____

_____

_____

_____

Friday: _____

_____

_____

_____

Saturday/Week-In-Review: _____

_____

_____

_____

_____

_____

WEEK 13

❦

Live a life by design! The best way to predict the future is to create it. You have the possibility to design your life any way you desire it to be. Place no limits on what's possible for you to manifest!

Jessina DeMarco

This week I live every moment designing what is the best life for me. I'm designing it the way it appears in my heart.

Monday: _____

_____

_____

_____

Tuesday: _____

_____

_____

_____

Wednesday: _____

_____

_____

_____

Thursday: _____

_____

_____

_____

Friday: _____

_____

_____

_____

Saturday/Week-In-Review: _____

_____

_____

_____

_____

_____

WEEK 14

❦

Realize that our thoughts in the first 20 minutes of our awakening moments are the most critical in the navigation of our day! Be sure to plant and cultivate positive thoughts and intentions in this precious space. This fertile ground will begin to produce fruitful outcomes!

Jessina DeMarco

I will focus this week on starting each day with meditation and intention on positive thoughts and feelings, which will design the outcomes that I experience each and every day.

Monday: _____

_____

_____

_____

Tuesday: _____

_____

_____

_____

Wednesday: _____

_____

_____

_____

Thursday: _____

_____

_____

_____

Friday: _____

_____

_____

_____

Saturday/Week-In-Review: _____

_____

_____

_____

_____

_____

WEEK 15

03

Say YES to Life, Say YES to Happiness, Say YES to You! You deserve all of the happiness and fulfillment that you desire.

Jessina DeMarco

I will open my heart to receive the greatest amount of happiness and fulfillment I desire, knowing that I deserve it all. There's no need for me to feel ashamed, in any way, to want any less than this. I AM worthy!

Monday: _____

_____

_____

_____

_____

Tuesday: _____

_____

_____

_____

_____

Wednesday: _____

_____

_____

_____

Thursday: _____

_____

_____

_____

Friday: _____

_____

_____

_____

Saturday/Week-In-Review: _____

_____

_____

_____

_____

_____

WEEK 16

☙

Live your tomorrow, Today! Your ability to see beauty and possibility is proportionate to the level at which you embrace gratitude!

Jessina DeMarco

This week I choose to live life in the present moment. My tomorrow is lived today and I enjoy being present at all times.

Monday: _____

_____

_____

_____

_____

Tuesday: _____

_____

_____

_____

_____

Wednesday: _____

_____

_____

_____

Thursday: _____

_____

_____

_____

Friday: _____

_____

_____

_____

Saturday/Week-In-Review: _____

_____

_____

_____

_____

ᵂEEK 17

☙

A great Life Partner is one who is already Whole. We are not here to complete anyone, but to merely add more value and happiness to their experience.

Jessina DeMarco

I am complete within myself! I choose to be the best partner I can be to my significant other. I choose to edify them and make their life experiences even more joyful.

Monday: _____

_____

_____

_____

Tuesday: _____

_____

_____

_____

Wednesday: _____

_____

_____

_____

Thursday: _____

_____

_____

_____

Friday: _____

_____

_____

_____

Saturday/Week-In-Review: _____

_____

_____

_____

_____

_____

WEEK 18

❧

I cleanse myself of all selfishness, resentment, critical feelings for my fellow beings, self condemnation, and misinterpretation of my life experiences. I bathe myself in generosity, appreciation, praise and gratitude for my fellow beings, self-acceptance and enlightened understanding of my life experiences.

Jessina DeMarco

This week will be a week of tremendous gratitude and self-love & care. I will continuously abide in days free of judgment and condemnation. I know that I am loved and appreciated and good enough all of the time.

Monday: _____

_____

_____

_____

Tuesday: _____

_____

_____

_____

Wednesday: _____

_____

_____

_____

Thursday: _____

_____

_____

_____

Friday: _____

_____

_____

_____

Saturday/Week-In-Review: _____

_____

_____

_____

_____

_____

WEEK 19

CB

True friendship should never come with contingencies! I love and accept you for who you are, right where you are!

Jessina DeMarco

I will begin to accept all of my friends and loved ones without any conditions. I fully accept myself, as well, without placing conditions on myself.

Monday: _____

_____

_____

_____

_____

Tuesday: _____

_____

_____

_____

_____

Wednesday: _____

_____

_____

_____

Thursday: _____

_____

_____

_____

Friday: _____

_____

_____

_____

Saturday/Week-In-Review: _____

_____

_____

_____

_____

_____

WEEK 20

ℭℬ

Raise your standards. Raise your expectations. Raise your minimums of what you will allow into your life that does not honor or respect you. Be bold, push the boundaries, and you will be rewarded!

Jessina DeMarco

This week I will focus on pushing myself to higher possibilities and standards. I will go the extra mile and dig a little deeper in every area, knowing that it's possible for me to achieve more.

Monday: _____

_____

_____

_____

Tuesday: _____

_____

_____

_____

Wednesday: _____

_____

_____

_____

Thursday: _____

_____

_____

_____

Friday: _____

_____

_____

_____

Saturday/Week-In-Review: _____

_____

_____

_____

_____

WEEK 21

❧

*Embracing the newness of life is such a beautiful thing!
Shedding away All that is non-serving and inviting in All that
is to our highest good. And so it is!*

Jessina DeMarco

I choose to focus this week on what is fresh in my life. I understand that my past doesn't belong in my future and I have the ability to bless it and leave it there.

Monday: _____

_____

_____

_____

_____

Tuesday: _____

_____

_____

_____

Wednesday: _____

_____

_____

_____

Thursday: _____

_____

_____

_____

Friday: _____

_____

_____

_____

Saturday/Week-In-Review: _____

_____

_____

_____

_____

_____

*W*EEK 22

☙

Life is not happening to you…Life is responding to you!

Jessina DeMarco

I know that I am the creator of my own future and destiny. I am proactive in creating this positive space that I'm in. I am not a victim of outward circumstances; they're just a reflection of what's going on inside of myself. I choose to feel empowered and blessed in my challenges.

Monday: _____

_____

_____

_____

Tuesday: _____

_____

_____

_____

Wednesday: _____

_____

_____

_____

Thursday: _____

_____

_____

_____

Friday: _____

_____

_____

_____

Saturday/Week-In-Review: _____

_____

_____

_____

_____

_____

WEEK 23

☙

As God IS, I Am! I inhale blessings and exhale gratitude!

Jessina DeMarco

I begin this week in a space of empowerment knowing that my creator supports me in every way. I give constant thanks and appreciation for all that I have now. I decide to live every moment of every day in complete gratitude and appreciation.

Monday: _____

_____

_____

_____

_____

Tuesday: _____

_____

_____

_____

_____

Wednesday: _____

_____

_____

_____

Thursday: _____

_____

_____

_____

Friday: _____

_____

_____

_____

Saturday/Week-In-Review: _____

_____

_____

_____

_____

_____

WEEK 24

❧

There are miracles happening all of the time! We must open our eyes and hearts to see them.

Jessina DeMarco

I will concentrate this week on all of the miracles that are taking place in my life every day. If it's a penny on the ground or an unexpected gift, I take notice to them all in tremendous gratitude.

Monday: _____

_____

_____

_____

_____

Tuesday: _____

_____

_____

_____

_____

Wednesday: _____

_____

_____

_____

Thursday: _____

_____

_____

_____

Friday: _____

_____

_____

_____

Saturday/Week-In-Review: _____

_____

_____

_____

_____

_____

WEEK 25

☙

I AM open and say "YES" to the people I'm supposed to meet and know about! Who we attract is in our energy and vibration!

Jessina DeMarco

I will take note this week of who I am attracting into my life. I know that like attracts like and I am surrounded with people who are of like-mind and I am attracted to those people as well.

Monday: _____

_____

_____

_____

_____

Tuesday: _____

_____

_____

_____

_____

Wednesday: _____

_____

_____

_____

Thursday: _____

_____

_____

_____

Friday: _____

_____

_____

_____

Saturday/Week-In-Review: _____

_____

_____

_____

_____

_____

WEEK 26

❦

Happiness is a choice, not a result. Nothing outside of you will make you happy. You must choose to be Happy!

Jessina DeMarco

This week I will give attention and gratitude to everything around me. I realize that my happiness comes from within, not from outside sources. Today I choose "Happy"!

Monday: _____

_____

_____

_____

_____

Tuesday: _____

_____

_____

_____

_____

Wednesday: _____

_____

_____

_____

Thursday: _____

_____

_____

_____

Friday: _____

_____

_____

_____

Saturday/Week-In-Review: _____

_____

_____

_____

_____

_____

WEEK 27

CB

Silence is golden! Some of the best conversations are held in it.
Silence is a place of great power and healing.

Jessina DeMarco

This week I will spend more time in meditation, prayer, and/or silent time with myself for the purpose of inner-reflection. This is my space and my time for me. I will listen and be open to the small voice that is within me for guidance.

Monday: _____

_____

_____

_____

_____

Tuesday: _____

_____

_____

_____

Wednesday: _____

_____

_____

_____

Thursday: _____

_____

_____

_____

Friday: _____

_____

_____

_____

Saturday/Week-In-Review: _____

_____

_____

_____

_____

_____

WEEK 28

☙

Our inner-work precedes and designs our outer-world! The Best gift ever is to show up for ourselves. Happiness is an inside job. Don't assign it to anyone else.

Jessina DeMarco

I realize this week that I create my own life experiences. The time and self-investment I spend in private is what will be manifested on the outside. I am Empowered and I am Happy!

Monday: _____

_____

_____

_____

Tuesday: _____

_____

_____

_____

Wednesday: _____

_____

_____

_____

Thursday: _____

_____

_____

_____

Friday: _____

_____

_____

_____

Saturday/Week-In-Review: _____

_____

_____

_____

_____

_____

WEEK 29

☙

I'm in so much gratitude for who I am today! I LOVE and ACCEPT myself unconditionally. I bless the lessons I've learned along the way that have brought me to where I am! Sometimes a short walk down memory lane is all it takes to appreciate where you are today!

Jessina DeMarco

This week I will focus on my past experiences. I realize that they are not mistakes, but lessons learned to move further on my journey today. If I do reflect back, it is merely to see where I've come from and give gratitude for who I am today.

Monday: _____

_____

_____

_____

Tuesday: _____

_____

_____

_____

Wednesday: _____

_____

_____

_____

Thursday: _____

_____

_____

_____

Friday: _____

_____

_____

_____

Saturday/Week-In-Review: _____

_____

_____

_____

_____

WEEK 30

❧

Fear is a human concept and a human experience! Love is infinite, with overflowing abundance! Choose to abide and reside in the place of Love!

Jessina DeMarco

I understand that love and fear cannot co-exist. This week and forever more, I act from the place of love instead of fear!

Monday: _____

_____

_____

_____

_____

Tuesday: _____

_____

_____

_____

Wednesday: _____

_____

_____

_____

Thursday: _____

_____

_____

_____

Friday: _____

_____

_____

_____

Saturday/Week-In-Review: _____

_____

_____

_____

_____

WEEK 31

❦

Lead from the front! A great example is worth more than a thousand words! Whether you know it or not, there is ALWAYS someone watching you! It's not what you say that is most reflective; it's what you do, which establishes true, enduring credibility!

Jessina DeMarco

I make every effort to live up to what I say, knowing that it is a direct reflection of my credibility to others.

Monday: _____

_____

_____

_____

_____

Tuesday: _____

_____

_____

_____

Wednesday: _____

_____

_____

_____

Thursday: _____

_____

_____

_____

Friday: _____

_____

_____

_____

Saturday/Week-In-Review: _____

_____

_____

_____

_____

_____

WEEK 32

❧

Appreciate today for the gift of stillness, and being present in the moment! The past is no longer in existence, and the future is not promised!

Jessina DeMarco

I choose today to live in appreciation and cease for the present moment, knowing it's the one thing I can never get back!

Monday: _____

_____

_____

_____

_____

Tuesday: _____

_____

_____

_____

_____

Wednesday: _____

_____

_____

_____

Thursday: _____

_____

_____

_____

Friday: _____

_____

_____

_____

Saturday/Week-In-Review: _____

_____

_____

_____

_____

WEEK 33

CB

Manifestations occur when your action steps are congruent with what you believe! Alignment must be present, otherwise it's work!

Jessina DeMarco

I make a conscious effort to take action in the direction of what I desire to achieve!

Monday: _____

_____

_____

_____

Tuesday: _____

_____

_____

_____

Wednesday: _____

_____

_____

_____

Thursday: _____

_____

_____

_____

Friday: _____

_____

_____

_____

Saturday/Week-In-Review: _____

_____

_____

_____

_____

_____

WEEK 34

❦

Love and embrace your beautiful journey! The first and most important person you can show up for is yourself!

Jessina DeMarco

I always place myself as the number one priority, so that I can be an even better blessing and light to those around me!

Monday: _____

_____

_____

_____

_____

Tuesday: _____

_____

_____

_____

_____

Wednesday: _____

_____

_____

_____

Thursday: _____

_____

_____

_____

Friday: _____

_____

_____

_____

Saturday/Week-In-Review: _____

_____

_____

_____

_____

_____

WEEK 35

☙

Know that there are no wrong paths that we have gone down! Every path we encounter will serve a high purpose on our journey! They will either teach us what we desire or what we don't desire! Either way, we are the better because of it!

Jessina DeMarco

I choose to appreciate all of my life experiences, knowing that it is either a win or a lesson learned!

Monday: _____

_____

_____

_____

Tuesday: _____

_____

_____

_____

_____

Wednesday: _____

_____

_____

_____

Thursday: _____

_____

_____

_____

Friday: _____

_____

_____

_____

Saturday/Week-In-Review: _____

_____

_____

_____

_____

_____

WEEK 36

ೞ

Silence your heart. Trust your inner-voice! Silence the outside chatter and always do what's right for You!

Jessina DeMarco

I decide to leave footprints of Love and Kindness wherever I go!

Monday: _____

_____

_____

_____

_____

_____

Tuesday: _____

_____

_____

_____

_____

Wednesday: _____

_____

_____

_____

Thursday: _____

_____

_____

_____

Friday: _____

_____

_____

_____

Saturday/Week-In-Review: _____

_____

_____

_____

_____

_____

WEEK 37

☙

Give what you want to receive! Kindness is a lifestyle!

Jessina DeMarco

I will make a conscious effort this week to deposit great things into other people's lives, as I would like for that to be reciprocated into mine. I will make this a new lifestyle for me.

Monday: _____

_____

_____

_____

_____

Tuesday: _____

_____

_____

_____

_____

Wednesday: _____

_____

_____

_____

Thursday: _____

_____

_____

_____

Friday: _____

_____

_____

_____

Saturday/Week-In-Review: _____

_____

_____

_____

_____

WEEK 38

❦

I AM my own unique self, special, creative and wonderfully made! I'm appreciating my beautiful creation!

Jessina DeMarco

I decide to embrace my uniqueness, knowing that I was created like no other, with my own fingerprint and uniqueness.

Monday: _____

_____

_____

_____

_____

Tuesday: _____

_____

_____

_____

_____

Wednesday: _____

_____

_____

_____

Thursday: _____

_____

_____

_____

Friday: _____

_____

_____

_____

Saturday/Week-In-Review: _____

_____

_____

_____

_____

_____

WEEK 39

☙

Trust and Be assured that everything is in alignment with your highest and best Good! Have faith that the changes you're experiencing are bringing you Blessings!

Jessina DeMarco

I choose to believe that all things are working out to my highest and best good, even when circumstances may not initially appear that way.

Monday: _____

_____

_____

_____

_____

Tuesday: _____

_____

_____

_____

_____

Wednesday: _____

_____

_____

_____

Thursday: _____

_____

_____

_____

Friday: _____

_____

_____

_____

Saturday/Week-In-Review: _____

_____

_____

_____

_____

WEEK 40

☙

True peace starts with oneself. When one has internal peace, it is projected out into the world, causing a ripple effect!

Jessina DeMarco

I intend on embracing inner peace, knowing that it will bring about peace to the people around me.

Monday: _____

_____

_____

_____

_____

Tuesday: _____

_____

_____

_____

_____

Wednesday: _____

_____

_____

_____

Thursday: _____

_____

_____

_____

Friday: _____

_____

_____

_____

Saturday/Week-In-Review: _____

_____

_____

_____

_____

WEEK 41

☙

Blessing the lives of others is the ultimate gift that keeps on giving! We are Blessed to be a Blessing to others!

Jessina DeMarco

I am always looking for ways to bless and bring light into others' lives. I will always be rewarded in many ways.

Monday: _____

_____

_____

_____

_____

Tuesday: _____

_____

_____

_____

_____

Wednesday: _____

_____

_____

_____

Thursday: _____

_____

_____

_____

Friday: _____

_____

_____

_____

Saturday/Week-In-Review: _____

_____

_____

_____

_____

WEEK 42

❧

Always look for the good in each person, situation and experience! Even if you initially can't rationalize the Why, know that everything is happening for a reason, that you are supported and things always work out in your highest and best interest. Our job is to simply surrender!

Jessina DeMarco

I will constantly look for the good in everything! This is a reflection of deep gratitude, a reflection of how I feel about myself.

Monday: _____

_____

_____

_____

_____

Tuesday: _____

_____

_____

_____

Wednesday: _____

_____

_____

_____

Thursday: _____

_____

_____

_____

Friday: _____

_____

_____

_____

Saturday/Week-In-Review: _____

_____

_____

_____

_____

_____

WEEK 43

☙

The way we start our day can affect our Whole day! Begin with a smile, joyful, at peace, a calm mind and much Gratitude!

Jessina DeMarco

I realize that the first 20 minutes of my day sets the tone for the entire day. I decide to cultivate thoughts that infuse happiness and serenity.

Monday: _____

_____

_____

_____

_____

Tuesday: _____

_____

_____

_____

_____

Wednesday: _____

_____

_____

_____

Thursday: _____

_____

_____

_____

Friday: _____

_____

_____

_____

Saturday/Week-In-Review: _____

_____

_____

_____

_____

_____

*W*EEK 44

☙

Each day is a gift and an opportunity to express our unique selves, to set aside perceived standards, and to break molds of mediocrity! We hold the paintbrush to create our own unique design and masterpiece. Be the YOU who's envisioned on the canvass of your imagination!

Jessina DeMarco

I WILL to operate in my bigger self! This person is the essence of infinite possibility.

Monday: _____

_____

_____

_____

Tuesday: _____

_____

_____

_____

_____

Wednesday: _____

_____

_____

_____

Thursday: _____

_____

_____

_____

Friday: _____

_____

_____

_____

Saturday/Week-In-Review: _____

_____

_____

_____

_____

_____

WEEK 45

☙

Achieving a dream is about more than just what we accomplish. It's about who we become in the process! Enjoy the journey! You'll be amazed as to whom you will discover!

Jessina DeMarco

I always focus on the journey more than the end result. I understand that who I become in the process is much more important than the destination.

Monday: _____

_____

_____

_____

_____

Tuesday: _____

_____

_____

_____

Wednesday: _____

_____

_____

_____

Thursday: _____

_____

_____

_____

Friday: _____

_____

_____

_____

Saturday/Week-In-Review: _____

_____

_____

_____

_____

_____

WEEK 46

☙

The past has already served its purpose. It is a place of reflection, not a place of residence! We have the choice to either use those lessons learned to propel us into our future, or allow them to keep us incarcerated to what is non-serving. One gauge that we are on the right path, is when we no longer care to look back!

Jessina DeMarco

I continue to focus on my beautiful future. I respect the past, knowing that it has molded me into the higher person I am today.

Monday: _____

_____

_____

_____

_____

Tuesday: _____

_____

_____

_____

Wednesday: _____

_____

_____

_____

Thursday: _____

_____

_____

_____

Friday: _____

_____

_____

_____

Saturday/Week-In-Review: _____

_____

_____

_____

_____

WEEK 47

❧

Believe that you are worthy of all that you envision and take inspired action towards it! 80% of SUCCESS is showing up!

Jessina DeMarco

I always ensure myself that I am valuable and deserving of all the dreams that I envision for myself.

Monday: _____

_____

_____

_____

_____

Tuesday: _____

_____

_____

_____

_____

Wednesday: _____

_____

_____

_____

Thursday: _____

_____

_____

_____

Friday: _____

_____

_____

_____

Saturday/Week-In-Review: _____

_____

_____

_____

_____

WEEK 48

☙

Those things that bring you feelings of happiness, gratitude, joy, peace, abundance, bliss; however that may show up for you, focus on that!

Jessina DeMarco

I only give energy and attention to things that bring great feelings to me. I know that whatever I focus on expands.

Monday: _____

_____

_____

_____

_____

Tuesday: _____

_____

_____

_____

_____

Wednesday: _____

_____

_____

_____

Thursday: _____

_____

_____

_____

Friday: _____

_____

_____

_____

Saturday/Week-In-Review: _____

_____

_____

_____

_____

_____

WEEK 49

❦

Believe and trust in the dreams that have been placed in your heart! They have been given to you for a reason!

Jessina DeMarco

I trust my intuition wholeheartedly and the vision that I have been given for my life.

Monday: _____

_____

_____

_____

_____

_____

Tuesday: _____

_____

_____

_____

_____

Wednesday: _____

_____

_____

_____

Thursday: _____

_____

_____

_____

Friday: _____

_____

_____

_____

Saturday/Week-In-Review: _____

_____

_____

_____

_____

_____

WEEK 50

Silence is Thunder! It is better to be quick to listen and slow to speak!

Jessina DeMarco

I decide today to use my words wisely. I will exercise compassion and an open ear to hear.

Monday: _____

_____

_____

_____

_____

Tuesday: _____

_____

_____

_____

_____

Wednesday: _____

_____

_____

_____

Thursday: _____

_____

_____

_____

Friday: _____

_____

_____

_____

Saturday/Week-In-Review: _____

_____

_____

_____

_____

WEEK 51

❧

The positive experiences that we impact on an individual can sing in their hearts for the rest of their life! Bring beautiful melodies to all interactions!

Jessina DeMarco

I let the sweetness of my being bring fruitful experiences to others, creating a ripple effect that goes a long way.

Monday: _____

_____

_____

_____

_____

Tuesday: _____

_____

_____

_____

_____

Wednesday: _____

_____

_____

_____

Thursday: _____

_____

_____

_____

Friday: _____

_____

_____

_____

Saturday/Week-In-Review: _____

_____

_____

_____

_____

_____

WEEK 52

☙

Staying in the place of gratitude and appreciation keeps me in alignment with ultimate happiness for who I AM, where I AM, and what I have right in this present moment!

Jessina DeMarco

I decide to live in the present moment, which is all the time I truly have. I understand that yesterday no longer exists, and tomorrow isn't promised to anyone.

Monday: _____

_____

_____

_____

_____

Tuesday: _____

_____

_____

_____

Wednesday: _____

_____

_____

_____

Thursday: _____

_____

_____

_____

Friday: _____

_____

_____

_____

Saturday/Week-In-Review: _____

_____

_____

_____

_____

_____

Being happy is the cornerstone of all that you are! Nothing is more important than that you feel good! And you have absolute and utter control about that because you can choose the thought that makes you worry or the thought that makes you happy; the things that thrill you, or the things that worry you. You have the choice in every moment.

~ Abraham Hicks

Self-Edification Exercise

List 10 Wins or Successes in your life that you are Honorably Proud of:
(Childhood, Adulthood, Family, Business Achievements, Health, etc.)

1) _____

2) _____

3) _____

4) _____

5) _____

6) _____

7) _____

8) _____

10) _____

Action Step: Make it a priority to say at least 5 of these each day out loud in a mirror, as part of your daily affirmations!

JESSINA DeMARCO

112

Delicious Daily Affirmations

- ❖ I AM, I Have!

- ❖ All things come to me with grace and ease!

- ❖ I AM positioned perfectly where I need to be. I AM right on time!

- ❖ I AM co-creating with Spirit!

- ❖ There are millions of ways that abundance will come to me!

- ❖ When I AM aligned, manifestations happen quickly and easily!

- ❖ I Let, not get!

- ❖ God IS, I AM!

- ❖ I give myself permission to be me!

- ❖ As soon as I ask, I receive!

- ❖ I AM open to miracles!

- ❖ I'm in the knowing that changing my thoughts creates a new reality!

- ❖ I love knowing that I have overflow!

- ❖ All is well, and is getting *weller*!

- ❖ I love and accept myself!

- ❖ My body is healthy, energized, and perfect in every way!

- ❖ I feel good and good is attracted to me!

- ❖ It's easy for me to express my needs and feelings!

- ❖ I deeply and completely love myself!

- ❖ I am winning the race of life!

- ❖ I easily attract love into my life!

- ❖ All of my relationships are loving and harmonious!

- ❖ I AM attracting emotionally available partners to my loving and giving spirit!
- ❖ I AM filled with energy to do all of my daily activities in my life!
- ❖ I AM perfectly healthy in mind, body, and spirit!
- ❖ My body heals quickly and easily!
- ❖ I AM in control of my health and wellness!
- ❖ I sleep soundly and peacefully!
- ❖ My mind is at peace!
- ❖ I always have enough money for all that I need!
- ❖ Wealth is pouring into my life!
- ❖ I pay my bills with love, knowing that these great companies are providing service to my life!
- ❖ I enjoy travel whenever I please!
- ❖ My passion is the Key to my abundance!
- ❖ I AM unified with the Universe!
- ❖ The Law of Attraction operates in my life for my highest good!
- ❖ Everything is getting better every day!
- ❖ I AM safe and always feel protected!
- ❖ I AM calm and relaxed in every situation!
- ❖ All is well in my world!
- ❖ I experience the excitement of growth today!
- ❖ It is easy for me to express my needs and feelings!
- ❖ I AM healthy and happy!
- ❖ I start great conversations easily and effortlessly!

- ❖ I approve of myself and FEEL great about myself!
- ❖ Every day, in every way, I AM getting better!
- ❖ I AM my own unique self, special, creative, and wonderfully made!

If you set goals and go after them with all the determination you can muster, your gifts will take you places that will amaze you.

Les Brown

Focus Wheel Exercise

Create a focus wheel around every aspect of life that you would like to affirm. The affirmation is inside of the wheel, the spokes will be all supporting statements that you wish to state to confirm this. Example:

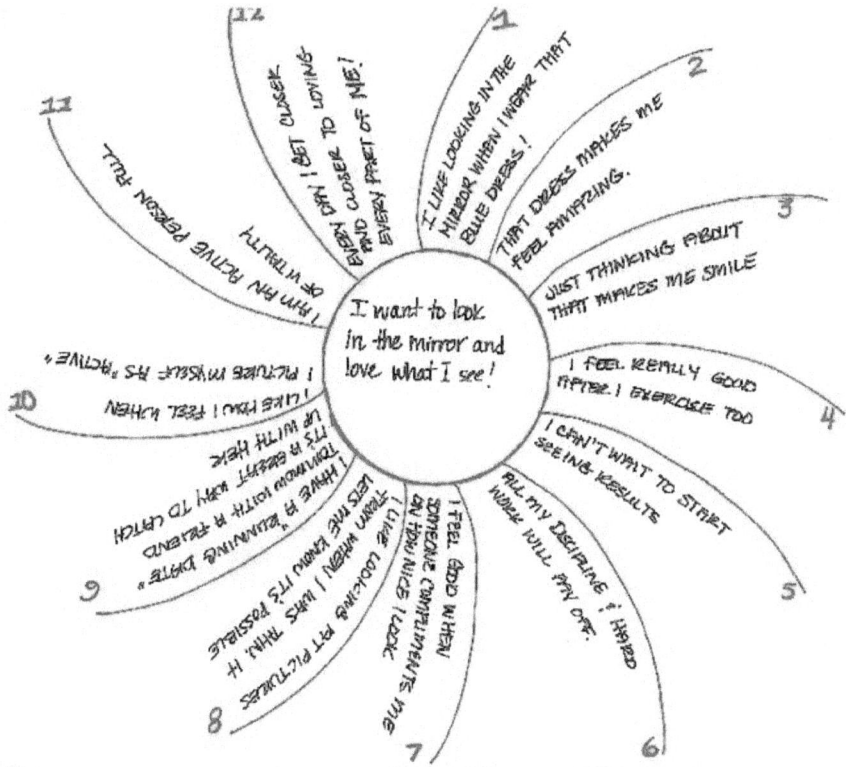

Center affirmation: *I want to look in the mirror and love what I see!*

Spokes:

1. I LIKE LOOKING IN THE MIRROR WHEN I WEAR THAT BLUE DRESS!
2. THAT DRESS MAKES ME FEEL AMAZING.
3. JUST THINKING ABOUT THAT MAKES ME SMILE
4. I FEEL REALLY GOOD AFTER I EXERCISE TOO
5. I CAN'T WAIT TO START SEEING RESULTS
6. ALL MY DISCIPLINE & HARD WORK WILL PAY OFF.
7. I FEEL GOOD WHEN SOMEONE COMPLIMENTS ME
8. I LOVE LOOKING AT PICTURES OF MYSELF WHEN I LOOK NICE!
9. IT'S EASIER TO WATCH MY DIET WHEN I PICTURE A FUTURE RUNNING WITH HER
10. I LIKE HOW I FEEL WHEN I PICTURE MYSELF AS ACTIVE, "ALIVE"
11. I AM MY MOST ATTRACTIVE PERSON OF WHEN I
12. EVERY DAY I GET CLOSER AND CLOSER TO LOVING EVERY PART OF ME!

Action Step:

Draw out these focus wheels and post or place them in an area where they will be displayed at all times, ever before you.

Resources

Listed below are reference materials and guides that I have found to be quite helpful and valuable on my journey:

- *STAND: Your Weekly Guide for Success*, by Ruben Mata
- *Money Made Simple & Delicious: 5 Keys To Having More Money Now*, by Marisa Nakhi
- *The Secret*, by Rhonda Byrne
- *If Not for the Grace of God: Learning to Live Independent of Frustrations and Struggles*, by Joyce Meyer
- *GOOD, BETTER, BLESSED: Living With Purpose, Power and Passion*, by Joel Osteen
- *LIVE YOUR DREAMS: Say Yes To Life*, by Les Brown

ABOUT THE AUTHOR

☙

JESSINA DEMARCO HAS BEEN SHARING HER PURPOSE in life and helping others for many years. She has been a Health and Wellness professional for over a decade, presenting a wealth of techniques and strategies for developing others to live a healthier life.

Jessina has earned licenses and certifications as a Massage Therapist, Master Neuro-Linguistic Practitioner, Master Success Coach and Certified Personal Trainer.

As a Health and Wellness professional, success coach/author, and an expert in success mindset, Jessina shows and teaches audiences how to create a new mindset around success, health and abundance

As an overcomer of many obstacles, she has learned to have compassion and understanding, and her purpose in life is to assist others on their journey to a more successful life!